Displays

Gary Beck

This publication is a creative work protected in full by all applicable copyright laws, as well as by misappropriation, trade secret, unfair competition, and other applicable laws. No part of this book may be reproduced or transmitted in any manner without written permission from Winter Goose Publishing, except in the case of brief quotations embodied in critical articles or reviews. All rights reserved.

Winter Goose Publishing
45 Lafayette Road #114
North Hampton, CA 03862

www.wintergoosepublishing.com
Contact Information: info@wintergoosepublishing.com

Displays

COPYRIGHT © 2015 by Gary Beck

First Edition, November 2015

Cover Art by Winter Goose Publishing
Typesetting by Odyssey Books

ISBN: 978-1-941058-36-7

Published in the United States of America

Tel qu'en lui-même enfin l'éternité le change,
Le Poète suscite avec un glaive nu.

Le Tombeau D'Edgar Poe—Stéphane Mallarmé

TABLE OF CONTENTS

9/11	1
The Coincidence of Birth	2
Confused Peace	3
Decline and . . .	4
Iraqi Conflict	5
Allocation of Resources	8
The Peril of Age	9
Liberty and Jus—	10
Home Security	11
Before 9/11	12
At All Cost	13
Unheard Arias	14
Material Questions	15
Art's Sake	16
Lead Us Not	17
e Equals . . .	18
French Conundrum	19
Tenement Trap	22
Mexican Vision	23
Sly Bigotry	24
Terror	25
Ars Brevis	26
Dependent Nature	27
Corrida in Palma de Mallorca	28
Poetry 2005	31
Ode to New York City	32
Sun	33
Manila Bay, 1898	34

The Electorate	35
Displays	36
Chess Master	37
E Pluribus	38
Survivor	40
Newton	41
Inquisition	43
Muse	44
Give Us Your . . .	45
Speculation	46
Aquatint	47
Comfort Zone	48
Fossils	49
Calculate	50
One If by Land	51
Stalk	53
Disasters	54
Withdrawn	55
Perspective	56
The Decline of Verse	59
Judgement	60
Distances	61
How to Know the Birds (an Introduction to Bird Recognition)	62
Rebuild	64
Three Visions	65
Sub	66
Pre-Dawn Slum	67
Montpelier, Vermont	68
False Alarm	69
Escape	70

Majorca	71
One World	72
Viewpoint	73
If Not Crusade?	74
Gold Fever	76
Cold War Fantasy	77
Cold War Truce	78
Paris	79
Morning Song	81
Friend or Foe	82
Next Time, Hurry	83
Early America	84
Looking Back	85
Ordinary People	87
Chant	88
Cynic	89
G Force	90
Toro	91
Mystery	93
Grow	94
I Am 27	95
Sparrow	96
Plea	97
War	98
Moon Over Vermont	100
Birth	101
Ebb	102
Fading Force	103
Central Park Zoo	104
Images of Three Cities	106
Politically Correct Terror	107

Do You Promise?	108
Ramble	109
Laughing Town	110
Relentless	111
Passage	112
Contagion	113
The Blessing	114
28	115
Consumer's Choice	116
Kaleidoscope	117
Loss	118
Neglect	119
Foreigner	120
Petit Scribblers	121
Mostly Ignored	122
Welcome Me, Tiresias	123
Epitaph	124
About the Author	126

"The poet must learn to expand his or her perception of existence and enlarge their scope of interest, or risk becoming inconsequential in this demanding life. There is an urgent need to reach out to diverse audiences, prisoners, seniors, the culturally underserved, and most important, to youth, not to make them poets, but to introduce them to a broader view of life. With proper instruction, poetry is the most accessible and cost effective way to reach large numbers of youth. The constriction of the classroom rarely develops confidence in youth, the quality that allows them to choose who they will grow up to be. The poet can help launch venturesome journeys for youth that will promote their contribution to the future of our society."

"Is the Poet Obsolete? The role of the Artist in Society"
—Gary Beck
Published by Poetic Matrix Press, 2009

*To poets anywhere who burn to speak to the world
of the issues of our times*

9/11

I heard the reading of the names
of the dead in the World Trade Center,
saw the faces of grief,
still feeling the pain of loss
that stole loved ones unexpectedly
when planes descended from the sky,
plunged into undefended buildings
completely unprepared for the attack
that forever shattered security,
since our finest efforts can't prevent
fanatic haters from striking again.

As Americans shared their sorrow,
some of us remembered the Arabs
dancing deliriously in the streets,
overjoyed at the death and destruction
suffered in the land of the free.
Yet Arabs mourn death of loved ones
as much as other people
and shouldn't be immune to our anguish.

Sorrow commemorated,
notable for resignation,
anger and outrage mostly faded,
the proud resolve of survivors
displayed the high ideals of our country,
still the democratic lamp of the world.

The Coincidence of Birth

I spent too much time in slums
to be deluded by mansions,
where offspring of privilege
protected from rude streets
get sustaining nutrition,
a secure base
for future ambitions.

Begrudged help for the needy
is insufficient for youngsters
born into the poverty class
without prior consultation.

I see the children of the poor
deprived of opportunity
because of their parents,
no fault of their own.

A just society
would insure all children
are included in tomorrow
with a fair chance
to build a fulfilling life,
contribute to the future.

Confused Peace

Unlike hawks,
doves are flock birds,
on close observation
quite violent.
The predatory hawk
operates alone,
except for a mate
is a solitary bird
with no flock urges,
only kills for food,
rarely attacks others,
lacks basic social skills,
content in nature
as long as man permits
the existence of nature.
Yet we've made the dove
a symbol of peace,
the hawk represents war,
confused labels
that lead us astray
from urgent questions
of war and peace.

Decline and . . .

Our brash exuberance is gone,
replaced with sober apprehension,
as the spirit that put men on the moon
has departed, leaving uncertainty.
We, the formerly opinionated,
eager to tell the world
how it should be run,
until the assault of terror
enhanced our economic doubts,
shook our faith, frightened us,
making some yearn for isolationism.
While we quiver in indecision
some are for war, some are against.
Once Americans spoke one language,
now divided by conflicting values,
not eager to assume tomorrows,
dwindled to ordinary people,
preoccupied with day-to-day affairs,
fearful of the future.

Iraqi Conflict

This morning I took the bus
to the village where I was born
to discuss events with the imam,
who has counseled me since childhood.
I told him of my confusion
since the Americans invaded.
They made all sorts of promises
if we didn't resist their attack
and like many of my Shiite friends
I left the army without fighting,
then our country surrendered.
There was little resistance at first,
despite infidel occupation
of our sacred Islamic land.
Then the cowardly flight of Saddam,
which meant the end of Sunni rule,
gave hope to my Shiite brothers
that we would be allowed to worship
in the glory of the one true faith,
no longer fearing persecution.
Sunni resentment was inflamed,
disorder threatened the land,
roadside bombs flourished like flowers
whose blossoms erupted in death.
The men of Al Qaeda arrived,
burning with zeal for destruction,
lusting to slay Americans,
or other foreign invaders.

Explosions became daily song.
There was talk of a new government
that would give us democracy,
but the son of the murdered El Sadr
aroused discontent in the poor,
hatred in the fanatics
against American soldiers,
and the new Iraqi government.
The sons and daughters of Iraq
became targets of terror,
and their deaths bring much sorrow.
My older brother joined the police
and was killed by a suicide bomber.

My sister became a translator
for the minister of education,
and was shot down in the street like a dog.
When I was summoned by Al Qaeda
to fight the infidel enemy,
I didn't know who was the enemy.
There are foreign occupiers,
the displaced loyalists of Saddam,
our powerless new government,
the cunning agents of Iran,
the treacherous men of Syria,
the bloodthirsty henchmen of terror,
and the smug people from the U.N.
I do not know who I should support.
I do not know who I should oppose.

Our respected religious leaders
do not speak out against the slaughter
of innocent Iraqi people,
simply trying to survive chaos.
Their exalted voices are silent,
so I visit a village imam
in the hope of obtaining guidance
to follow the will of Allah,
in a time of terrible troubles.

Allocation of Resources

Street crime in America,
according to *The New York Times*,
is supposed to be down, down, down,
and citizens should feel safer.
Yet acts of extreme violence
are becoming commonplace,
making many of us inured
to once unacceptable horrors.
As our prisons grow more populous
than some of the world's nations,
we should consider the lost resource
of men idly sitting in their cells
serving unproductive sentences
who might be enlisted
with appropriate protections
for our society
for public service,
a chance for redemption.

The Peril of Age

Political inclinations
that generally conflict
sometimes become more moderate
when youthful passions are tempered.
There are exceptions,
primarily senility,
which makes us querulous
and impatient of another.
There is loss of appetite,
and the struggle for clarity
makes it hard to remember
what the effort is all about.
Fatigue is a tranquilizer
that erodes the will for combat,
drains perseverance
that provided satisfaction.
The worst condition of old age,
is when we're too numb to care
what happens to the world at large,
because it no longer matters.
Loss of transmission of knowledge
from one generation to the next
causes dumbing down of our country,
threatens the future of youth,
who may not be smart enough
to insure continuation.

Liberty and Jus—

American troops died in Iraq
month after month following the conquest,
a feat of arms comparable
to Germany's defeat of France.
Iraqis, however, are not Frenchmen,
and lacking western civilized ways
were willing to suicide themselves
to resist encroaching democracy.
Politicians in our homeland quibbled,
while our youth's blood stained desert sands.
Some of our more extreme citizens
accused our president of war crimes,
a charge normally presented
by the nations that hate us.
Conspiracy theorists complained
that we were waging a war for oil,
while they bought bigger SUVs.
Journalists weakened our will to act
by invoking the dreaded specter
of the quagmire of Vietnam.
In this softer, more liberal age,
it's unreasonable to expect
public approval for blood-and-guts war,
but there should be recognition
for the sacrifice of our troops
who suffered and died
to create democracy.

Home Security

I sit on my terrace in safety
with doves and finches for company,
still protected by my government,
still able to dream tomorrows.
I am not alone in privilege.
Many of my countrymen
still have jobs, homes, possessions,
with reasonable assurance
they will continue existence
for the foreseeable future.
As the tide of strife and destruction
sweeps across the vulnerable world
we are frequently endangered
while our system of democracy,
despite endless shortcomings,
provides some of us with comforts.

Before 9/11

Before 9/11
most Americans
didn't think much about terror,
those who did
assumed it confined
to the troubled Mid-East,
other third world countries
that we looked down on.
The public didn't expect
the horrific attack
that leveled the Twin Towers,
murdered our innocents.
Now the fear of terror
is not far from the thoughts
of concerned citizens
who do not sleep as soundly
while Al Qaeda still lurks
in caves of malice
plotting death and destruction.

At All Cost

Bursts of radiation
dangerously dispersed
destroy communities,
unless regulated
to protect citizens.
Unlawful release
of nuclear weapons
in a contracting world,
makes all of us suffer
the same consequences.
It is debatable
whether the bombs
dropped on Hiroshima,
dropped on Nagasaki,
were truly recognized
at the time they were used
as inhumane weapons
of mass destruction,
making many of us fear
that nuclear weapons,
proliferating,
impose a threat
that shouldn't be ignored.

Unheard Arias

The purple finch and house finch
are unappreciated
by busy city dwellers,
who never take the time
to listen for a moment
to their melodious song
that would please receptive ears,
otherwise deafened
by city commotion.

Material Questions

Buildings of brick or stone
admit insufficient light
to alter the resolution
demanded by commerce.
Buildings made of glass
test the commitment
of lowly workers
to resist distraction
from the views of freedom,
and remain diligent
in repetitive tasks.
Buildings of metal
dazzle the viewer,
but contain employees
who rust away unnoticed.

Art's Sake

Once bright young men
in this great republic
grew up quoting heroes:
Don't fire until you see . . .
Don't give up the . . .
We have just begun . . .
Nowadays bright young men
cluster on street corners,
heads encased in earphones
digitally bellowing
unprecedented filth,
socially accepted by many
as approved cultural products.
Of course we never defined
exactly what is our culture,
and self-appointed elites
have neither taste nor wit
to clarify for bright young men.
Those who applaud at the opera
before the aria is even finished
are no different than vulgar rappers,
both seeking to establish value
in the eyes of their neighbors.

Lead Us Not

Perfection is a fantasy
foolish minds babble about
when less rooted in reality,
or absorbed in escapism.
At our best we often err
and failings are more extensive
than taken-for-granted virtues.
Goodness is less exciting
than squalid titillation
demonstrated daily
in media presentations
of arson, rape, assault, robbery,
and nothing appeals as much
as a marriage-ending murder.
We spectate with as much delight
as patrons of the Roman Games,
diverted from daily problems
by unscrupulous tyrants
exploiting human nature,
making us constantly struggle
against temptation
that summons moral decay.

e Equals . . .

Adrift in the chaotic universe,
I urgently need to maintain control
of some elements of existence
that challenge my trivial power.
As my planet speeds through its orbit,
I barely cling to the surface,
pressured by every kind of force,
especially that of gravity.
I fear eco-disaster everywhere,
see man's best creations wasted in war,
yet precisely align my dresser drawers
in a mostly futile effort
to establish a sense of order.

French Conundrum

La Belle France,
most fickle of allies,
or committed oppositionist,
possibly once a true,
if albeit flighty friend.
What did we do
to alienate you?
In your war with England
for possession of the new world,
so what if we sided with England.
After all, we were them.
And you did send nasty Indians,
who scalped our women and children.
Then in Revolutionary War times
you supported us against the English,
although it was more to thwart them,
rather then to really help us,
but we didn't resent you.
When revolutionary fervor
removed a large number of heads
from aristocratic shoulders,
we didn't publicly deplore
your Gallic excess.
We may have compelled Napoleon,
to make the Louisiana Purchase,
which we cleverly manipulated,
before there was a law of eminent domain.
So what if it was a swindle.

Business is business,
whether French or American.
Didn't you try to sneak a king next door,
in Mexico of all places,
despite the Monroe Doctrine,
thinking we were too busy to notice
in our preoccupation with the Civil War?
If we righteously reined in
your imperialism in China,
we said nothing about the rest of Asia, or Africa.
We saved your empire in World War I,
but you never forgave us our youthful power.

You never forgave us World War II,
when we liberated your occupied country
and Le Grand Charles never forgot.
And if that wasn't grudge enough
to build eternal animosities,
smack dab in the early days of the Cold War,
while we were getting shellacked in Korea
you got whomped in Indo-China
and of course couldn't forgive us
for not nuking the Viet Minh.
There was dancing in your streets
when we got zapped in Vietnam
and ever since our ignominious defeat,
you take enormous pleasure
in any of our setbacks,
military or political.

We can only regret
that your stubborn ways
blind you to the overwhelming need
for the services of the good old USA,
the next time you're in trouble.

Tenement Trap

Generation after generation
have smoldered relentlessly
within your bile-green walls.
Italian, Jewish, Black, Hispanic,
all indiscriminately
filled the air shaft with refuse,
protesting their coffin confines.
The dirt-encrusted windows blend
changing seasons into one entombment
of thwarted hopes or expectations,
crushed by the scurry of rat and roach feet.
No wonder so many of your children,
arbitrarily consigned to squalor,
rejected the feeble offerings
of a disdainful society
and encouraged by embittered parents,
turned their abilities to crime.

Mexican Vision

Maria Sanchez,
daughter of a land of sun,
whose body never loved by water
begins to lose its juices in the heat.
Ah, Maria of the tears,
your husband's gone across the border.
Are your thighs lonely?
Do they sing to lusty men
who pass your doorstep in the evenings?
Ay, Maria,
the good Virgin understands.
She will send your husband home with wealth,
or not at all.

Sly Bigotry

The black men of my city
used to walk the dawn streets
in constant anger.
They did not fear
the nighttime men in pale sheets,
but wilted under the slow sneer,
patronizing hand,
bad joke, nervous glance,
but all that changed
after 9/11,
when democratic death collected,
regardless of race, creed, color.

Terror

International terrorism,
an inhumane condition
whether Islamist or narco,
is still granted civil rights,
but shouldn't conflict with self-defense.
After all, even to liberals
survival should be more precious
than outrage at a backpack search.
It's convenient to cry conspiracy
when some suggest
forces of law and order
oppress their citizenry
with arrests and seizures,
yet demand protection
when sudden detonations
explode tranquility.
Living in a state of siege
is not the optimum consideration
for fulfilling the American dream
but we should be aware
that World War III is underway
and immediately invite
nations that prize freedom
to join us in resisting
the enemies of our civilization.

Ars Brevis

Culture clutchers
no longer sustain themselves
from the rude assault
of omnipresent rap.
Practitioners of the monotonous beat
are too aggressive
for fragile followers
of delicate arts.
The future of ballet, drama, painting
will ultimately be decided
by the raucousness
of street performers.

Dependent Nature

The struggle for survival
compels all living creatures
to accept harsh reality,
eat or be eaten.
Only mankind defies the laws
that govern earthly existence
by inventing new devices
for protection from disaster.
Vulnerable creatures
can't adapt to rapid change,
are inevitably doomed
to extinction of species,
or dependency on man
for continuation.

Corrida in Palma de Mallorca

Pressed against the aging gates
of the Plaza del Toros,
impatient American sailors
clutching colorful, overpriced tickets,
purple and green contrasts
against the white of summer uniforms,
mouthing vile curses,
thinking no one understands English,
sneered at by Mallorchinos,
wisely waiting in the shade, resentful,
but knowing that the ships will soon depart.
An ugly, comic spectacle.
Then the opening of the gates.
The hawkers waiting rank on rank,
loudly screaming the praises
of sombreros, cushions, fans, cerveza, Coca-Cola,
pursue the sailors with relentless cries.
The public climbs to seats,
half the arena in the shade,
the other half in la sol,
echoing with the pleas of hawkers to buy
matador hats, picador hats, flamenco hats, any Spanish hat.
Buy, buy, buy,
bulls' horns, tails, ears,
as cheaply made as the hats.
The arena slowly fills to the chorus of hawkers,
who the sailors curse and mock,
as they never would in their own land.

A water truck enters the arena,
sprinkling the ground to settle the dust.
The band seated high in the shade begins to play.
The procession enters,
more vain than dignified,
more arrogant than proud.
Bows, applause, struttings, a trick horse.
Then the first bull.
Even the sailors stop cursing.
The toreadors excite the bull with capes
and quick retreats to safety.
Enter the picadors carrying lances,
grotesque on padded, blindfolded horses.

The bull, tormented by capes,
is led to a picador,
who stabs him with his lance.
Lowering his horns,
the bull charges the picador,
trying to gore through the padding.
Then the matador enters,
without throwing his hat to a beautiful woman,
crosses himself
and signals everyone to leave the ring.
The crowd applauds. He faces the bull,
calls gently: "Hola, Toro."
The bull paws the earth, charges,
is gracefully evaded.
A dozen passes. The crowd olés.
He works the bull adroitly.

Another pass. Stumbles,
falls against the bull's head,
between the horns.
The crowd falls silent.
Toreadors rush into the ring.
He recovers and waves them away.
Another pass and turning his back on the bull, walks off.
He places the bandilleras himself,
alone in the ring with the bull,
skillfully, two at a time: two, four, six.
The crowd screams olés.
Then the kill.
On tiptoes,
sighting the fragile-looking sword between the horns,
one smooth lunge over the head
and the bull is dead.
The crowd roars olés.
The matador circles the ring, bowing.
A yoke of horses drag out the carcass.
Sand is scattered on the blood.
Appetites whetted,
the crowd awaits another death.

Poetry 2005

The guardians of poetry,
mostly self appointed,
produce polished products
that make their universities proud.
Don't all poets go to college now?
Somehow they've managed to convince
a non-discriminating public
that form is more important than content,
style more necessary than substance.
The endless hordes of versifiers,
mostly sustained by academia,
have subtracted the elemental fire,
constrained the extremes of emotion,
removed the excess of fervor,
provided well-constructed poems
as substitutes for passion
that make poetry a desert sameness,
elegant, remote, serene,
infinitely arid.

Ode to New York City

Cultural, financial capital
of the rapidly narrowing world,
streets formerly designed
for horse and carriage
teem with experience seekers
avidly recording
with digital cameras
everything they see.
Despite media exposure
of crime, drugs, poverty, discourtesy,
visitors are amazed
at the kindness of New Yorkers,
who were that way before 9/11,
but now are more appreciative
of day-to-day niceties
binding us together in troubled times.
Our tolerance is unpublicized,
despite the patience we maintain
when protestors abuse our right
to host democratic events
in relative peace and tranquility,
simply because they disagree with us.
They are not patriots versus loyalists,
southerners versus northerners,
merely transient summer soldiers
fervent for disruption,
offering no alternative
but commotion
and we'll quickly forget them
during clean up.

Sun

After many days of cold rain
august Vermont began to dry
despite loud complaints
from sundry birds
that had not helped.
But sometime after lunch
the sun broke through
tease of clouds
keeping things wet and chilled
and shined just long enough
to factory whistle to work
bees, flies, gnats.

Manila Bay, 1898

Into your tropic harbour
in shimmering motion
sailed the upstart ships,
intent on conquest.
Your aging armada,
a rusting relic of empire
still hoping to possess you,
was compelled to action,
and couldn't resist the onslaught
of vigorous new masters
intent on acquisition,
sinking all objections
in the grin of victory.

The Electorate

In democratic America
the two party system
has reached the point
where many citizens,
mostly of liberal persuasion,
have forgotten our privileged state
allowing free elections,
and will righteously accuse
those who disagree with them,
exercising their right of choice
selecting a third party alternative,
of betraying their beliefs
by rejecting their candidate.

Displays

Rapid transmission of information
generally disturbs the tranquility
of citizens going about their business,
hoping to avoid demands
on limited attention spans.
Before the advent of TV
it took a while for daily news
of death, disaster, destruction,
to reach readers, or listeners,
with details of recent horrors.
Once upon a time
murder could be committed
in relative obscurity.
Wars and invasions were waged
without public supervision.
Every kind of crime and abuse
was mostly carried out in private.
Then portable TV cameras
proliferated throughout the world
and endless hordes of eager peekers
poked their avid lenses everywhere,
recording the most dreadful acts
of man the destroyer.
Now the visual displays
of our varied iniquities
have not modified behavior,
merely made some of us
pathologically eager
to flaunt evil for an audience.

Chess Master

Chess master,
twisted by the board of life,
a predatory hustler,
hulking in chess shop lairs,
dormant until prey appears.
When a stranger enters,
greasy eyestalks calculate
the volume of his treasure.
Only suckers pass inspection
and are admitted to camaraderie,
for as long as they will play and pay . . .
Fifty cents a game . . .
The master's way.

E Pluribus

In the great experiment
rejected ingredients
from foreign laboratories
combined arbitrarily,
without scientific method
and miraculously produced Americans.
It was an imperfect process.
Nevertheless, the results were . . .
historically unique.
Diverse elements united,
however different constituent parts,
mostly without use of force,
and incorporated in a system
that functioned fairly well.
Then time took its inevitable toll
and corruption outweighed idealism,
suspicion replaced public trust,
separatism became condition normal,
other languages began to supplant English.
Citizens were no longer content
to just be Americans
and were African-Americans,
Hispanic-Americans,
and the fabled dream
was measured by money.
Alienation became our way
and the hope of mankind's future
is engaged in competition

with an awkward entity,
The European Union,
another confused entrant
for a melting pot future.

Survivor

Going north to Vermont
on Route Seven,
somewhere in the twilight
in the Green Mountains,
the road spirals up and round
down into darkness,
headlights snaring
a lonely felon,
a deer.
Violet eyes of fright
blaze before her flight.
She made it this time.
She was beautiful, wild, free,
much wooed by fenders.

Newton

Newton, home from college
(because of plague)
suffered severe restrictions on his activities,
because plague was mighty contagious
(mostly fatal)
and people thought it undesirable,
behaving badly to those who caught it,
(consequently)
to relieve the boredom of small town life,
(subsequently)
invented calculus at the age of twenty.

He didn't waste time marching to ban gunpowder
and had no patience with those who cried *get out of Europe*,
he knew what kept the big, bad Continentals away.
(And as the myth goes)
Was sitting beneath an apple tree
(you fill in the next line).
....
Now people had been watching apples fall
a long, long time
(Neanderthal saw apples fall.
Adam saw apples fall.
The clever Greeks saw apples fall),
but no one figured out why.
So where would we be today
if we protested fire,

Displays

banned the wheel,
cried: *get out of Gaul?*
We might be marching for civil rights
of underprivileged creatures
from Proxima Centauri.

Inquisition

When dreaded Torquemada
made insistent inquiries
designed to elevate, liberate,
spirit from flesh,
beneficiaries were referred
to the appropriate claims office
in the vain hope
of future settlement.

Muse

Tyrants never commission
small statues, small paintings,
preferring dominant display
of larger than life images
that constantly intimidate
in public spaces.
Visual surveillance
reminds subject people
they must maintain
respectful demeanors.
Despite concluding
conspirators are too cautious
to gather under watchful eyes
of Uncle Joe, Popa Doc,
secret police remain alert
for undesired criticism
of the artistic taste
of self-appointed leaders.

Give Us Your . . .

Immigrants once
were welcomed
to our accepting shores
and didn't fear the secret police
unless they ran afoul of them.
After a strained interlude
citizenship is acquired,
the next generation
go about their business
with rights and privileges,
except those previously reserved
for members of the oligarchy.
Illegal aliens, however,
are not desirable guests
invited to visit,
let alone permanently reside,
and the clamor of pressure groups
to enfranchise illegal entrants
abuses the principles
of our besieged republic.
We are entitled to determine
who we do, or do not want
residing in our land.
Despite Latino sympathy
for drybacks across the border,
we should regulate admittance
to the fraying American dream.

Speculation

Shades of regret
quickly interfere
with timely recognition
of immoral acts.
We lose hope
of redemption
if we don't differentiate
between various degrees
of right from wrong.
With all our talk of afterlife,
some of us are still not sure
if consciousness survives death,
allowing continuation.
For those who lack certainty,
reason will elevate our hopes,
nature will release the beasts.

Aquatint

Often stormy China sea
whispered by pungent ghosts
adrift on lost junks,
fifty ancestors deep,
harboring mysteries of decay.
British sailor, 1880 imperialist old,
riddled with pox . . .
Relics of rubber empires,
(blind to Tai Mountain)
opium nights,
brotheled wenches of churning hips,
(yellow brother plots and schemes)
then home after eighteen years,
(no more lizards on the ceiling)
and Cora runs off with a gun-boat officer.
Waterfront gutter drunk,
singing raucous whiskey songs . . .
of youth . . . a woman . . . unsyphilitic love . . .
a teardrop of filth
washed across exotic maps . . .
China sea.

Comfort Zone

Decay is inevitable
for organics,
and humans qualify
with peculiar penchant
for ossification.
Yet we shouldn't lament
demise of our creations,
which are not roads to eternity,
but temporary way stations,
devised by a clever species
to assist needy travelers
on confusing journeys.

Fossils

Long before creatures
obligingly crawled
into ice, earth, stone,
to become fossils
determined to seek
life after death,
there were no speculations
of science and religion.

Calculate

Disinclination for improvement
results in sterile accomplishment,
generally indicates
declining capabilities,
a not abnormal occurrence
of growing loss of interest
in challenges of life.
Continuation of existence
measured
by a personal calculator
assesses the degree
of effort exerted
to sustain the future.

One If by Land

Slothful America
awakened
to the terror jolt
on 9/11
that shocked us
out of complacency.
Many quickly forgot
the urgency of fear,
reverting to old habits
rather than recognizing
implacable threats
menacing our survival.
Fanatic terrorists
professing belief in Islam
invoke the word of god
to justify destruction
of infidel enemies,
while practitioners
of the same faith
refuse to reject
desecrators of the Koran.
At odd times in history
there have been instances
when those not with us
were definitely against us,
but in our overcrowded world,
despite instant communications,
miracles of science,

charitable assistance,
most inhabitants
remain helpless victims
of hunger, poverty, disease,
and are really not enemies.
The specter of religious war
obscures greater human needs
than doctrinal differences
that should not be tolerated
by men of faith.
We do not know if anarchy,
spearheaded by Bakunin bombers,
would have been defended
by the ACLU,
but when bombs go off
on our vulnerable streets,
murder our children,
we must confront
the polarizing conclusion
that war on terror
may be our only choice.

Stalk

Silence is the stealthy stalk
in forest clearings
that hush the warning hisses
from ravenous paws
that from concealment pad
intent on pausing a creature
from survival cares.

Disasters

Fortunate survivors
often reminisce
about horrors escaped,
frequently confusing
capabilities
with good luck.
Time and distance
cloak traumatic events
in vague remembrances,
diverse interpretations,
fading perceptions,
leading us to conclude
despite preparations
for dangerous situations
the appearance of chance
may result in salvation.

Withdrawn

Inertia is an erosive
seeping purpose from the will,
leaving the isolated self
too clogged to seek redemption.
A greater act of will
opposed to forces of dissolution
can reactivate the spirit
slumbering beneath the surface,
waiting for the call to action.

Perspective

There was a brief interval
after World War II
when future expectations
dazzled us with possibilities.
America the privileged
used global conflagration
to emerge from isolation
and its legions triumphed.
The mechanisms of war
were highly profitable,
suffering minimal damage
America became mighty.
But democracy didn't understand
how to regulate conquests.
First we rebuilt Western Europe,
then we rebuilt Japan,
assuming in our puppy way
they would be our friends
and forget how we destroyed them.
We packed up most of our troops,
shipped them home to civilian life,
while the Russians refused to leave
countries they occupied
and the world was divided
into two opposing camps.
It took a while for America
to learn the war we thought we won
wasn't really over.

Our erstwhile ally, now our foe,
was challenging our non-empire
and once again we were called to arms.
But times had drastically changed
and Uncle Joe and his Cossack hordes
oppressed the lands they occupied,
while our men had shed their uniforms
and enrolled in college.
Millions of our citizens
suddenly had a real chance
for the hitherto fabled life
only to be found in books or films,
and they had more to lose
than drafty peasant huts,
barely sustaining diets.
Many of our citizens,
overburdened with possessions,
became too uncomfortable with war,
at least if they had to fight it,
and resorted to time-tested methods
that offered our underclasses
as cannon fodder,
while the well-to-do stayed home
and learned how to play golf.
Fortunately for our republic
there has always been a supply
of belligerent young men,
ready, willing, and eager
to rapidly become trainable
to confront our enemies
with gun, bomb, bayonet.

Nowadays we're lucky
that young women have the chance
to kill our enemies,
because no matter how much
some of us yearn for peace,
the world is unequally shared
and greedy men and women
always seek more wealth,
more power, more goods
at the expense of others.
Avid accumulators
of the fruits of wealth
will always guarantee
the absence of tranquility.

The Decline of Verse

Emotional eunuchs guard
the portals of poetry
and arbitrarily judge
who is allowed to enter.
Armed with weapons of style,
they have forgotten substance.
In the safety of college
they are immune to the struggles
that consume mankind daily
and prefer metaphor
to unadorned statement.
They never wonder
why people no longer feel
a thrill reading poetry.

Judgement

Let us fervently hope
no scales weigh
the good actions of man,
compared to evil deeds.
The balance would tip
against salvation,
for the evil we do
eclipses our feeble good.

Distances

N.Y. ...........................L.A.
Paris...........................Peking
Washington...................Moscow
Earth..........................Moon
Me.............................You
You........................... Me

How to Know the Birds (an Introduction to Bird Recognition)

Finding myself far from city concrete
in the Green Mountains of Vermont,
listening to many birds, even seeing them,
thought how nice to learn about birds.
Bought a book. Told me:
North America has 650 species.
Robins wouldn't practice miscegenation.
One out of every six birds is a warbler.
A creeper climbs trees upwards in spirals.
Had listened to a bird sing:
Here comes the bride.
Dubbed it the marrying bird,
saw it performing solemn ceremonies in forests.
Turned out to be the white-throated sparrow,
yup, sparrow, and it was really singing:
"Old Sam Peabody, Peabody, Peabody" . . . Who he?
But it was a real poetic bird book.
"The laugh of a loon on a northern lake
is like the mirth of a maniac."
I found out the marrying bird,
confirmed blue jays and the hairy woodpecker,
so got my money's worth.
Found out that in the East
are five kinds of brown thrushes.
They all go through Washington DC.
Won't say anything about ducks,
'cept the ruddy duck,

which is the only ruddy duck
can't walk on ruddy land.
Always liked sea gulls,
found shouldn't call 'em sea gulls.
Always hated pigeons,
found they was doves.
Found a line:
"When warblers surge northward in May
bird watchers reach yearly climax."
Guess I've read enough for now.
Can't find the bird that gloats: I'll tell your mother,
but have it on authority that jays are crows,
and so intelligent they will dispute the earth with
dolphins,
when Man is gone.

Didn't mean to interject
a sour note into bird thoughts,
but panic over precise identification
of warblers and sparrows
ended this rumination.

Rebuild

When purpose is lost,
mental, emotional, physical
decay is inevitable,
unless urgent steps are taken
to rapidly regenerate
old attitudes into new goals,
despite obsolete mechanisms
that conspire to prevent
improved functioning.

Three Visions

I am the sleepless dreamer
gathering accolades from rooftops.

Whether in my land, or another,
the houses are mostly dark
before midnight.

With eyes closed,
anywhere in the world,
I am not more a stranger
than with eyes open,
anywhere in the world.

Sub

In Big II, the cruise began
with a surface run
that ended not too far from Pearl,
and sliding down not too deep,
trusting to ping and scope
to find a juicy target crosshaired,
waiting for a fish.
A carrier was too good to be true
and the torps ran bad at the big tanker
and couldn't catch that Mogami class
and the tin cans wouldn't let us near the troopships,
but with a little luck, plenty of skill,
the necessary ration of guts,
we did the job, sat out the depth charges
and got home again to base,
racks empty, broom high.
Then out again,
until Tokyo Bay ended our sweeps.

Pre-Dawn Slum

The dreams and visions of the poor stare hungrily from haunted eyes. Unremitting toil is etched upon an aged and weathered brow. Memories pass the ranks of elders seated on the stoops in the flashing bodies of unbeaten youth. And above the tenements a flame flickers, while men lie abed and cannot sleep. At three a.m. the streets are silent, save for passing autos' plaintive whines and clicking footsteps of a night-wanderer. The lost sea-cry of lone boats on the river rends the night and rents the heart, and late into the sleepless night men yearn for voyages to romantic gulfs or adventurous seas. Tall smokestacks belch grey plumes, covering the neighborhood with gritty, pungent filth. The tenements of time stand eerily tinted by cold streetlights. Buildings passed a thousand times in daylight are foreign, making this any street in any land. The filth and decay seen in the daytime is obscured. All that's visible is the chronicle of life, etched in blood, on cracked and rotting walls.

Montpelier, Vermont

Pollution is forbidden in the Winooski River,
but no one seems to remember that men
have driven on uncongested moon highways.
Not many folks seem myths of New England.
Prognathic jaws, rickets, beri-beri, scurvy,
Sunday blue law VD, much sinus trouble
and watery eyes from the gold dome capital,
dazzling with Doric exterior.
Haven't seen Corinthian interior; won't.
Not much more than Main Street,
but most of America
is not much more than Main Street.

False Alarm

Doves and hawks dispute
whether we should have peace or war.
The doves call the hawks brutes.
The hawks call the doves wimps.
Historically, war seems to be
a constant of society,
Americans rarely remembering
that most of our wars were by choice.
The endless Indian wars,
Mexican-American, Spanish-American,
World War I, II, Vietnam, Grenada,
Gulf War I, Afghanistan, Iraq,
all avoidable
with sufficient citizen objection
to resorting to force of arms
to settle disputes.
Maybe we had to fight 1812,
and probably Korea,
but that leaves a lot of wars
subject to question,
suggesting that Americans
are ready, willing, eager to fight,
as long as they're allowed
decent intervals
between battles.

Escape

If I were a fish
wouldn't like to be American.
Polluters and anglers
would take years off my life.
I'd like to swim secure,
so I'd find some deep,
bathysphere repelling sea place
and bring my wife
and do the best I could
to bring the kids up decent.

Majorca

Go up the mountains to Valdemossa,
where other tourists certainly have gone
to see where George Sand and Chopin lived,
she smoking her cigars,
he coughing into handkerchiefs.
It is not difficult to picture them,
she flaunting herself before Spanish eyes,
outraged by her trousers and impudent ways,
he delicately covering his mouth,
softly sighing at the turmoil of their days.
How innocent in retrospect they seem
in our time of decadent indulgence.

One World

Mankind's differences
are still more important
to the bulk of humanity
than any similarity of need.
The lack of thought
allowed most men
to ignorantly conclude
it's only coincidence
we share the same planet.
As the world grows smaller,
dimmer, more hostile to survival,
we don't have a long term plan
to insure existence
of a destructive species
risking redemption.

Viewpoint

I couldn't become
a certain type of birdwatcher,
snug in safari coat,
burdened by binoculars,
peeking, prying, poking,
until hated by every bird.
Not being an ornithological voyeur,
but respecting positive identification,
I found myself thinking about
indigo bunting, scarlet tanager
on tropical migrations.
I won't do malice aforethought spying,
but will keep eyes peeled.

If Not Crusade?

The vocabulary of terror
entangles our lives,
as newer foes
presume to inherit
the stature of Cold War enemies,
who except for suiciders,
are not entirely unlike
renaissance banditi
lurking in isolated places
practicing depredations,
then slinking back to obscurity
when destruction completed.
Twenty-first century media
fan the flames of violence
with instant worldwide communications,
graphic visuals that reinforce
the horrors of detonations,
while mainstream Muslims are silent,
except to infidel overreactions.
Muslims may not have a pope
to speak for one religion,
but that doesn't mean the many voices
of self-appointed Mid-East presidents,
generals, colonels, mullahs, imams,
other self-proclaimed dictators
of the heritage of Mohammed,
should allow abusers of the faith
to kidnap the word of god
and carry out abominations in his name.

Throughout the Cold War,
the United Nations General Assembly
generally assembled and was hostage
to two conflicting powers,
or third world manipulations.
Now that the Soviet Union is no more,
the big, bad U.S. of A.
has inherited all the fear, resentment, hatred
that once was shared with the big, bad bear.

We are now engaged in protracted war
that could become a clash of civilizations
if responsible Muslims don't respond
to the anarchic excess of extremists,
if western societies don't recognize
the threat to their institutions,
if the U.N. doesn't defend
mankind's aspirations.

Gold Fever

Gold rush race,
use any means, else too late.
Greedy yellow metal dreams
ebb away in tarnished streams,
flowered hills, twinkling rills.
Hunger, scurvy, gunshot
ends the claim
to golden fame.

Cold War Fantasy

Although the Japanese and Soviets
are slaughtering whales unchecked
and only the men of the good old U.S. of A.
are conservationally concerned,
'cause competition never good for business,
nevertheless, one day,
Nips and Ivans will get theirs,
when Polaris rears her proud head.

Cold War Truce

I swam in a tiny swimming hole
in a chilly Vermont stream
and after the first goose-bump tremors
never felt so fine
and couldn't recollect
in recent crises
when I had no imminent thoughts
in a body of water
of Polaris surfacing.

Paris

Legend across the ocean,
language, history, culture,
older houses, streets, cafés,
distant as church antiquities
spreading venerable thighs to tourists,
clicking cameras at palaces and whores.
Americans on the grand boulevards
complaining of prices and rudeness,
watch people carry long, slim breads,
as urgent for home as in other lands.
Little withstands the praise of guidebooks.
The Louvre, mostly filled with weary art.
Egyptian, Greek, Roman, unstirring
in a restless age of atom visions;
countless shallow paintings praising France,
perhaps a dozen works to kindle passion.
The rush to Mona Lisa, ignoring De La Croix.
Not quite dismembered as de Milo, Louvre,
shrine, immortal pause . . . dreary moment.
Urinals, Le Metro, bookstalls on the Seine,
the winding mystery of unfamed streets.
Spanish music from a closed café
breaking the morning silence in Monmartre,
students begging francs in St. Germain.
The butchers sleep on benches by Les Halles,
fingers twitching for their cleavers.
And more police
than any city under siege.

Exiles always came to you,
till airfare to New York became cheap.
Dream city, no refuge, still delight.

Morning Song

The animals of man,
dog, cat, roach, rat,
guests, invaders,
have been replaced
by the chorus of machines
singing the songs of dawn.

Friend or Foe

We no longer think of your U-Boats
surfacing in frigid seas,
welcoming our offspring with torpedoes.

We've already forgotten your aircraft
swooping down from the rising sun,
kissing our sons with tracers.

We barely remember your endless, quilted hordes
marching from Asian depths,
greeting our children with U.S. steel.

In each bitter war
our patriotic armies met the enemy,
sweltered, bled, blistered, froze,
obeyed their orders,
and joined the hallowed dead.

Next Time, Hurry

Old man winter
creeps in fast one day,
sneaking a feel
of frightened girlie earth.
She collapses in a cold faint
and the old guy's fastest lust
falls upon her sprawled thighs.
She cries: "No! No!"
But the old guy sneers,
tugging at his shiny trousers,
saying: "I know what you need, cutie."
She sighs, tired of struggling,
covered by her unheeding mate.
The old fool, spent too soon,
is lulled to doze.
A sly shift, a swift shove,
and just then,
faster than a speeding bullet,
the sound of hooves and a hearty
that punk spring,
better late than never.

Early America

Ripped from virgin woods,
conned from redskins,
coveted by many
of the imperialistic establishment,
Dutch, Swedes, French, British, Spanish,
and Russians always sniffing at the back door.
We bluffed and bought,
took and traded,
fleeced and fought,
until we brought forth a new nation.
We never stopped eyeing, groping, snatching,
found ourselves pretty big one day.
despite a civil war
that didn't prevent
our always reaching
for a larger country.

Looking Back

When I was a boy
people weren't any better
than their counterparts today,
just more self-controlled.
They committed outrageous crimes,
though not so regularly,
cursed, fought, raped, killed,
just not as frequently
as present day perpetrators.
We didn't have
constant TV news
live and in color,
enhancing every assault
on the public sensibility,
until our values frayed
from pictorial intrusion
into our daily lives.
Each lurid detail
of every vicious attack
on children, women, men,
shown over and over,
dissolves our attention span,
encouraging us to forget
recurring horrors.
Now we face instant opposition
to any effort that restricts
the rights of citizens
(even non-citizens)

from their opportunity
in the land of the free
to commit hideous crimes,
then not be put to death,
allowed to live
(often in more comfort and stability
than before they went to prison),
while their victim's dreams
have been extinguished.
In the endless struggle
between freedom and constraint
we have learned that profit corrupts
as much, or more than power,
necessitating laws
that should be enforced
to protect the people.

Ordinary People

People in the South Bronx
are like people in the North Bronx,
or any other place.
If you look behind skin deep,
you'll find preconceptions
that have judged, condemned, sentenced
the undefended to exile
in the slums of fate.

Chant

Who are we, that with deathless words
should sing of visions we invent.
Had we the wisdom that we presume,
we would be silent, awed by our finity,
but as church voices chant a prayer
to someone who is, or is not there,
we too shall hymn ascensions.
We are motes in the universe,
whose fleeting moments quite reverse
the magnitude of exile
upon our boasted speck,
remote from other life forms,
orbiting the galaxy
that finds us bold sailors,
embarked on vast journeys.

Cynic

Someone harbouring
nothing but derision,
eroding potential joys
that time could bring,
yet may still flourish
if scorn is replaced
with urgent seeking
of improved tomorrows.

G Force

Gravity's got me down,
trapped me in its pull.
I tried to free my soul,
but it gripped me to the ground.
Each time I would fly up
it pulls me down,
but ever up again,
as long as life, breath, motion,
makes me soar, swoop,
gull crude, loud, flight proud,
borne by heavy self
that carries me aloft,
each time prolonged,
catapulted beyond
action, or inaction.

Toro

The death-blood smell stenches the air.
I do not want to go.
They force me through the little gate.
I run into the center of the ring,
where the smell of one I know rises
in bitter fumes that frighten me.
How can I get away?
The men are there
and make sounds at me
and wave large, noisy arms.
I run away,
but there is no way to leave the ring.
An evil smell is in the air.
I run at them,
but not too close.
Do they think I want to fight?
It is sticky hot in the sun
and the lingering breeze
builds me dreams of home
and the cool river of evening.
Why is that man sitting on the horse?
Aieee. He stuck me with the something sharp.
I feel the hot blood running down my back.
The flies gather for a tasting.
A man tears off his hat and throws it in my face.
I run. How can I show them my friendship?
The noise of screaming men deafens me.
Why is that boy pointing his shiny stick?

Aieee. It has pierced my innards.
I stand frozen.
The men yell and wave at me.
I am falling, falling, falling,
remembering the cool river of evening . . .
Remembering the cool river . . .
Remembering . . .

Mystery

The light of other lives
burns behind shaded windows,
always duller than imaginings.
We still retain the secret hope
that hidden from our prying gaze
there still beats an eager heart,
not yet resigned to loss of dreams.

Grow

Without regret or hesitation,
though fearful of stumbling,
farewell all those who slay you
with love's blinding, sweet caress,
with need's urgent, blunt demand,
with passion's touch of wild stirrings,
the easiest drought of oblivion.
The lonely cry, or selfish claim
has many ways to strangle
a vulnerable fool,
entombing yourself in enticements.
Without backward glance, pause,
though dwelling in error,
farewell everything that binds you,
farewell your failing self.

I Am 27

Here I am,
27 years old,
sitting on a park bench,
dreaming of nothing.
The old man nearby,
one tooth in his head,
remembering glories,
has more dreams than I.
With all my power,
bursting with purpose,
swollen with longing,
I remain inert,
while the old man still cavorts.

Sparrow

Surely the sparrow
is more fragile
than I am,
yet it survives another day
by nature's grace,
as do I.
In the struggle to exist
I remember that frail bird
and hope I will endure.

Plea

About as far west as we can go,
until we reach the coast highway,
then Catalina, or Aloha,
deep into the deceptive Pacific,
where western man,
having always gone west in lust,
to explore, fight, take, settle
a piece of land, any desirable place,
has run out of direction, except up,
or down to the temporary sea solution,
now requires Congress, or someone
with purse, power, vision, who knows
if we don't expand, we contract.
Having grown as personal free
as possible in temporary abode,
a fine young land
surely has a future
on distant G-type stars,
lonely for men.

War

Evening church bells sound the hours
in dreary rooms just faintly lit
by dim candlelight that glowers
in corners where the parents sit.
Then the guest arises, starting
homeward, his smile and bow of head
soon will ease the ache of parting
and warm the virgin to her bed.

Fleeting moments of order.

But then the boots begin to march,
and the wheels begin to rumble
while in dread young men's throats would parch,
as old men began to mumble,
about the glories of their youth,
forgotten was their fear when led
to wars that always hid the truth:
What glory when the young lie dead?

Then the armies numbered millions.

Never again the old men swore
so many of our sons were slain.
We shall not make another war
and always women sobbed in pain.
So men rebuilt their homes and town
and women made new sons to show

the world's wonders and win renown,
but old hatreds began to grow.

Tremors felt in many lands.

The boots began to march again.
The wheels rumbled even faster.
The speed of aircraft blinded men
to the menace of disaster,
unleashing a wild destruction
on the world that was unprepared
to heed voices of instruction
from the sensible few who dared.

Twisted in postures of madness.

How long before protest works? Time
refused to wait until reason,
destroyed by man's unholy crime,
withdrew to await her season.
Men, too busy killing to mourn;
in prisons, battles, tortures, bled
in millions, a new age was born,
with nations numbered in the dead.

Ovens to end people,
bombs to end cities.

Moon Over Vermont

Had to really struggle to get
the Montpelier, Vermont, restaurant
to turn on the TV at nine thirty a.m.
to see the Apollo 15 Moonride.
Thought I missed the LEM descent,
but as the TV focused in, saw
the incredible hop to surface
of Dave Scott. Thought of Conrad, Armstrong,
Aldrin, others who left footprints, debris,
man stuff I hope I someday see.
Greatest show on earth.
Then Jim Irwin hopped down,
while Warden orbited round and round.
Finally the moon convertible,
just when Detroit's dropping that line,
drove off into the moonscape,
the finest ride man ever made.

Birth

Into the blindness of man-child birth, hurled
as fast as fingers grasp the waiting world,
fugitive from womb's protective haven,
without omen bird; eagle, hawk, raven,
to signify prophecies of promise
of empires, glories, visions, not to miss
wisdom, step-child of imagination,
eclipsed by vanities of ovation.
Springs into life clutching clots of birth blood,
senses awakening in rampant flood
that delivered a victim to exile,
who is forced to survive the first trial
with gore, howl-cries that torrent elation
from the awed birth-magic of creation.

Ebb

I shall not wander far again,
just sit at home and breed old age,
while all my passions roar with rage,
I'll live fantasies now and then.
I will sit in dull remembrance,
a prisoner of past delights,
leave present hopes for ancient sights,
an old dream of heroic stance.
This fading man, this ebbing force,
a stranger to my lustless eyes,
lingers a brief moment, then flies,
ending self's seeking at its source.

Fading Force

This time so filled with remembrance
of beggar's words that seem to prance
from my dishonest mouth's story,
that struts a moment of glory,
laments its defeats in despair,
chants of maidens with streaming hair,
who slay their hopes and change their ways
the victims of my maddened days,
that pass as swift as spring's delight,
that stir me in a blaze of white
flash-fire, extinguishing the coals,
mocking my unaccomplished goals.

Central Park Zoo

Indoor cages, the winter cells
of pacing felons,
condemned for life,
for being caught, or born.
No friends outside to plan a break.
"Daddy. Daddy. Buy me peanuts for the elephant."
Snarl, screech, whine, waiting
for the keeper's careless moment,
the moment that never comes.
"Don't put your hands there, honey. He might bite you."
They watch the man things pass from cage to cage,
gaping, laughing, teasing with idiot sounds,
yokels at a sideshow entertainment,
diversion from tortured creation.
"Do you want hot dogs and popcorn, kids?"
The monkey house of human convolutions,
doomed to acrobatics and lice picking.
No parole board reviews these cases.
Lions, tigers, panthers, eat exile's meat,
flung by lordly keepers,
while blood of distant jungles
screams for stalk and kill.
"He likes me, Daddy. I just know he does."
Bewildered bears not fooled by rocks and pools.
Cafeteria, dreariest cage of all.
Smaller animals sleeping, or scurrying,
without the aura of fierce beasts,
penitentiaried by man's cunning.

"Daddy. Buy me a balloon."
The hippos in their bathtubs,
the elephants of entertaining trunks,
yak, camel, bison, elk, moaning and shitting,
patchworks of fantasy, or fading beauty.
"Daddy. Why can't we take him home with us?"

Images of Three Cities

<u>Paris</u>
For those born too late for enchantments,
demons never seem to whisper here,
only old crones posed upon embankments
mechanically mumbling in their fear.

<u>Munich</u>
The church towers with their ghostly clocks,
rise through the haze of evening piety,
like vague and distant peaks of ancient rocks
that make their claim on eternity.

<u>Geneva</u>
The streets are always as clean and cold
as the snow on Mont Blanc, year round,
that beckons tourists who are told
where Switzerland's pleasures will be found.

Politically Correct Terror

Educated Westerners,
flirting with belief, or disbelief
in various religions, philosophies,
other spiritual, intellectual diversions,
frequently arrived at an ethos;
live and let live.
Radical Islam
has no tolerance
for anything it disagrees with
and urges political application
of death and destruction
to all unbelievers
and their infidel ways.
A peculiarity of our country
is that Moslem fanatics
seething with hatred of the West
can threaten our cities with fire,
murder our sons and daughters,
behead helpless captives,
while we are forbidden
to call for crusade
against unrelenting terror.

Do You Promise?

No more talk of patient dreams
our lives have churned to madness.
Relentless as a tartar horde
we sack the village of our souls.
Briefly we ignite the drowsy world,
while incendiary shadows strip us bare,
we fall into each other's flesh
till we expire in cooling cinders,
wipe the remnants of our love
on torn and grimy towels,
face each other from alien planets,
bear false witness to this fading life,
then move apart.

Ramble

People not having (nomore) conversations
mitt Gott,
(praps they took one a dem pleasure boats to the Bahamas,
an you knows what happens ta them)
neverthelesslessless . . .
Psych men swear
they got answers,
(but)
who's got questions?
Now
(if they wore eerie masks
and threwmysteriouspowders
in to fire)
depressing is repressing,
we got fears enough
without paying
(a helluv a lot)
for them to find more,
zo—
not having good advice
to give gratis,
the post office stopping
my soliciting cash thru gov't mails,
(zom noive!)
I remain,
Faith . . .
Yr, hmbl. obdt. servt.

Laughing Town

If I would go traveling down
the rock-strewn path to laughing town,
that lies within the mountain's shade,
that falls upon a sunless glade,
where boys of youthful hunger mass
to watch the lithesome virgins pass
that flirting place, the township's square,
filled with folk from the summer fair.
If I would go traveling down
the steep-sloped path to laughing town,
I'd surely find a maiden there,
who shyly strolls the township square,
with blushes turning cheeks to wine,
if her dreamful gaze should meet mine.
If I would go traveling down
forbidding paths to laughing town,
some wondrous things of rare delight
would surely pass before my sight,
had I dared go traveling down
torturous paths to laughing town.

Relentless

If we would touch tomorrow's woes
a fleeting gesture with our toes
to pause a moment's candy cry
from babes who briefly bloom then die,
before the hour of each is told
with faint fury whimpering soft,
they pass from blaze of youth to old
penitents, hurling words aloft.
When is their moment? Then they brood
that ambition will never slip,
releasing its relentless grip,
leaving heirs to beatitude.

Passage

Rumors that the light within men's eyes
is the soul's light, that blazes, flickers, dies,
suddenly and so soon that scarce a youth
survives to learn time's enduring truth.
Are we fragile bits that easily surrender
a part of us to troubles that can render
us weak in our eyes, or our brother's?
We are too fearful of the stares of others.
Do only children wonder why
it is so difficult to laugh or cry?
We linger as strangers a moment,
possess nothing, with dreams unspent,
leave our place in trembling fear
we never have existed here.

Contagion

Those who do not fear
the sudden attack of terror
have not been exposed
to the instant shock,
the paralyzing dread
of unexpected assault.
The intent of terror
by dedicated haters
who have opted to destroy,
rather than build,
is the fracturing of stability
in organized society.
Advanced civilizations
require order
to develop, maintain
complex structures.
Terror disrupts
more than tornado, earthquake,
which at least remind us
we are vulnerable to nature.
Terror doesn't educate, illuminate,
merely destroys the targets
of envy, fear, hatred
by the dispossessed,
who have renounced
humanity.

The Blessing

Go forth into tomorrow
speaking of creation.
Softly touch another's vision.
Do not pause in backward glances,
hungering for make-believe,
failing to catch enchantments.
Build an altar to acceptance
praising each moment of journey,
seek a special beauty of your own.

28

Now, when I am 28 years old,
and my work has really not begun,
to be forgotten is a fear
not half so great as never being known.
So brief a time so quickly spent
in play, work, love, countless dreams,
but king of all, smirking in triumph,
the specter of waste,
reckoning victories on many fingers.

Consumer's Choice

A couple of years ago,
media reported big scandal,
warning attentive viewers
we were getting excrement
in our burgers.
Never having developed appetite
for that kind of stuff, ceased.
Gradual evolution of hunger,
excrement, or other stuff
discovered in other meat,
brought me back to medium-rare,
onioned and ketchuped,
questionable protoplasm.

Kaleidoscope

Odysseus,
prurient bastard,
ugh.
How many Trojans, master,
lubricate thy vassals?
Help. They would slay the king afoot.
Marry, maiden, don't beget,
thy mate will make thy favours wet.
Who doth approach?
Ken you not?
We shall sack libraries,
blaspheme often,
swill cocktails,
partake of Polo.
Chukker, chukker.
Ha, knave. Would'st have yon dwarf?
He will lay thy wife upon her back.
Be warned. No woman can resist his hump.
Fire . . . Burpburpburp.
Calling lunar expedition.
Do you read me?
The old man's calm. Come home.
Have your coffee,
morning journal,
tablet of repentance.
Asia stirs.
Omens.
How many years?

Loss

Daylight fading in the war-torn west,
the only inn a lice-filled nest,
with goods, woman, apprehension,
paused the night
and thought of morn
and brave men's scorn,
saw the eyes of her I loved
rounder with illumination grow,
as my fear began to show,
then lost forever love's delight
as I displayed such craven fright.

Neglect

Too busy with tomorrows
I fear I'll never make,
that let me ease your sorrows
and slowly let you break
and fade away inside your shell
and doom you to a silent hell.

Foreigner

Needy stranger,
impale yourself
in someone else's flesh,
seem to mesh,
then spin apart,
further than the empty heart.

Petit Scribblers

In the nineteenth century,
passionate poets,
Byron, Pushkin, Whitman,
affected thousands of readers
and enriched their lives.
In the twenty-first century
thousands of poets,
academically nurtured,
do little more than divert
hundreds of readers
who rapidly forget
slick, unstirring poems.

Mostly Ignored

Poor Auden. "Spotless rooms
where nothing's left lying about
chill him," and so do other
important things: He swears
he warms to stable sort of stuff,
that makes him feel trés
secure, because he can sneer,
in a sneaky way.
The consonant mumblings
of his sensitive stumblings
stir up a storm of somnolence.

Welcome Me, Tiresias

Fueled by endless failures
in every aspect of my life,
I struggle with the paradox
of exercising faith without belief.
I never focused my desires
on material prosperity,
consequently, am not entitled
to complain about the absence
of expensive possessions.
I'm certainly not surprised
that my passionate efforts
to serve the needy, write, create,
contribute meaningfully
to a decaying culture,
have met rejection,
yet I continue to persevere
in the elusive expectation
for hope of amelioration
in the discouraging future.

Epitaph

Here lies someone born and bred
to be a victim, always led.
His days were brief,
his deeds were few,
he was perhaps like all of you.
Think when this epitaph is read,
are you alive, and is he dead.

Poems from *Displays* have appeared in: *A Hudson View Poetry Digest, Adagio Verse Quarterly, Alura Quarterly, Ampersand Poetry Journal, Ann Arbor Review: International Journal of Poetry, Arabesques Review, Autographs Magazine, Autumn Leaves, Avocet, Bathyspheric Review, Blackmail Press, Blueprint Review, Bolts of Silk, Calliope Nerve, ChiZin, Chronogram Magazine, Common Sense 2 Journal, Decanto Magazine, Defenestration Magazine, Eighty Percent Magazine, Em Dash Literary Magazine, Feathertale Review, Foliate Oak Literary Magazine, Fret Punch, Global Tapestry Journal, Greens Magazine, Hemingway's Shotgun, Holy Cuspidor, Hulltown 360 Literary Journal, International Zeitschrift, Journal of Truth and Consequences, Lesser Flamingo, Madswirl, Menda City Review, Mirror Dance, Motherkisser, Near East Review, Noneuclidian Café Journal, Phati'tude Literary Magazine, Pink Mouse Publications, Poesia Literary Quarterly, Poet Express, Poetry Cemetery, Poetry:stet, Puffin Circus, Rattlesnake Review, Shine Journal, Silent Actor, Spokes, Star*Line Magazine, The Bad Futurist, The Custer-Hawk Gazette, The Golden Lantern, The Houston Literary Review, The Verse Marauder, The Write Place At The Right Time, Tinfoil Dresses, Velocities, Wolf Moon Journal, Yippee Magazine.*

About the Author

Gary Beck has spent most of his adult life as a theater director. He has had numerous published works including *Days of Destruction*, *Expectations*, and his novel, *Flawed Connections*, published by Black Rose Writing. Gary has also had several original plays and translations produced off Broadway, in New York City, where he currently resides.

www.ingramcontent.com/pod-product-compliance
Lightning Source LLC
Chambersburg PA
CBHW051345040426
42453CB00007B/417